I0605378

KNOW THE FACTS

THE FACTS ABOUT Vaping

Carla Mooney

San Diego, CA

About the Author

Carla Mooney is the author of many books for young adults and children. She lives in Pittsburgh, Pennsylvania, with her husband and three children.

For more information, contact:
ReferencePoint Press, Inc.
PO Box 27779
San Diego, CA 92198
www.ReferencePointPress.com

Picture Credits:
Cover: Oleg GawriloFF

6: Aleksandr Yu/Shutterstock
10: Bruce VanLoon/Shutterstock
13: Andrey_Popov/Shutterstock
16: FabrikaSimf/Shutterstock
20: Attasit saentep/Shutterstock
23: Jorge Elizaquibel/Shutterstock
25: Pikselstock/Shutterstock
29: richard mittleman/Alamy Stock Photo
32: Gorodenkoff/Shutterstock
35: SB Arts Medea/Shutterstock
40: Monkey Business Images/Shutterstock
43: Hurricanehank/Shutterstock
45: Monkey Business Images
49: PL Gould/Shutterstock
52: Jonathan Weiss/Shutterstock
55: SIPA USA/Alamy Stock Photo

LIBRARY OF CONGRESS CATALOGING-IN-PUBLICATION DATA

Names: Mooney, Carla, 1970- author.
Title: The facts about vaping / by Carla Mooney.
Description: San Diego, CA : ReferencePoint Press, 2026. | Series: Know the facts series | Includes bibliographical references and index.
Identifiers: LCCN 2024054273 (print) | LCCN 2024054274 (ebook) | ISBN 9781678210465 (library binding) | ISBN 9781678210472 (ebook)
Subjects: LCSH: Vaping--Juvenile literature. | Electronic cigarettes--Juvenile literature. | Teenagers--Tobacco use--Juvenile literature.
Classification: LCC HV5740.5 .M66 2026 (print) | LCC HV5740.5 (ebook) | DDC 362.29/6--dc23/eng/20241226
LC record available at https://lccn.loc.gov/2024054273
LC ebook record available at https://lccn.loc.gov/2024054274

CONTENTS

INTRODUCTION

A Vaping Habit

G Kumar started vaping as a student at the University of Colorado. Flavored disposable vapes were popular among university students, and Kumar became one of many young adults who experimented with them. Soon, Kumar was vaping every day. Before long, Kumar needed to vape multiple times to get through the day. The vape pen always had to be within reach, or Kumar would go on a panicked search for the device. "It needs to be right next to my head when I fall asleep at night, and then in the morning, I have to thrash through the sheets and pick it up and find it,"[1] Kumar says. Even when Kumar got sick with COVID-19, the college student refused to put down the vape pen.

Eventually, Kumar, who is now twenty-four, decided to quit vaping. Kumar quickly discovered that quitting the vaping habit was not easy. The young adult picked up some quitting aids from the university health center, including two boxes of eucalyptus-flavored toothpicks. Although the toothpicks did not taste good, they helped whenever Kumar wanted to vape. "The fact that I could just gnaw on toothpicks for weeks on end was, I think, what kept me sane,"[2] Kumar says.

Many people find themselves in a situation like Kumar's. They tried vaping for a variety of reasons but now find it difficult to stop the habit. "Everyone knows it's not good for you, and everyone wants to stop. But at this point, doing it all these years . . . it's just second nature now. They're hooked on it,"[3] says University of Colorado senior Jacob Garza, who works to raise awareness about vaping as part of the school's health programs.

A Popular Pastime

E-cigarettes were first invented in China in 2003. Since then, they have quickly become popular worldwide. E-cigarettes have many names, including vapes, e-cigs, vape pens, and vaporizers. All are electronic nicotine delivery systems. In vaping, users load e-cigarettes with cartridges that hold a liquid that contains nicotine, flavorings, and other chemicals. E-cigarettes have a heating element that heats the liquid until it becomes a vapor. Users inhale the vapor into their lungs, where the nicotine and other chemicals are absorbed into the bloodstream via the lining of the lungs.

"Everyone knows [vaping is] not good for you, and everyone wants to stop. But at this point, doing it all these years . . . it's just second nature now. They're hooked on it."[3]

—Jacob Garza, a University of Colorado senior

In recent years, vaping has become a popular alternative to smoking tobacco. Nationwide, 6 percent of US adults aged eighteen and older regularly used e-cigarettes in 2023. Users can experience the buzz and adrenaline rush from nicotine without the stigma and smell of smoking cigarettes.

Controversy Persists

Despite its increasing popularity, vaping is controversial. Supporters insist that vaping is less harmful than smoking, which is a long-established public health problem. They argue that e-cigarettes can play a valuable role in helping smokers quit and preventing people from starting to smoke.

However, critics point out that vaping also carries health risks. Preliminary studies have linked vaping to several health issues, including heart and lung damage. Some people have experienced life-threatening reactions to vaping. Also, vaping delivers a concentrated dose of nicotine, an addictive chemical that can negatively impact the body and brain, especially in teens. Many are concerned that e-cigarettes are creating a new generation of

Vaping is a popular alternative to smoking tobacco. Users inhale nicotine-containing vapor from a device called an e-cigarette.

young people addicted to nicotine, which may be a gateway to smoking and other substance use.

In 2018, US surgeon general Jerome Adams responded to a significant increase in teen vaping, declaring it a public health epidemic. At a press briefing with Adams, Secretary Alex Azar of the US Department of Health and Human Services warned the country about the dramatic increase in teens and young adults using e-cigarettes. "We have never seen use of any substance by America's young people rise this rapidly. This is an unprecedented challenge,"[4] said Azar.

In the years since, vaping has remained a serious public health concern, particularly among teens and young adults. In 2024, e-cigarettes were the most commonly used tobacco product by US youths, according to the Centers for Disease Control and Prevention (CDC). Nationwide, 1.63 million students actively used e-cigarettes. More than 25 percent of youth users admitted to vaping daily, and nearly 40 percent reported using e-cigarettes at least twenty days during the past month.

Currently, there is a lot of conflicting information about vaping. Scientists are still gathering information about the long-term health effects of vaping and the effectiveness of e-cigarettes as a smoking cessation tool. Governments around the world are also debating what regulations, if any, are needed for e-cigarettes and related products. Policies aimed at reducing youth vaping may create barriers for adult users to quit smoking, which is a potentially harmful outcome. Since e-cigarettes have only been sold for a relatively short time, much is still unknown. Most vaping supporters and critics can agree on one thing: more research is needed.

CHAPTER ONE

An Alternative to Cigarettes

Freelance musician Liam Mallon first started smoking traditional cigarettes around age fourteen. For Mallon, smoking was part of family life; his father, mother, and grandmother all smoked. He remembers his grandmother offering him a puff on her cigarette when he was about seven years old. Once Mallon started smoking regularly, he quickly became addicted. "Tobacco was easy to get a hold of and relatively cheap back then, so buying a pack of cigarettes per day became routine for me,"[5] he recalls. Like many smokers, Mallon smoked to relax and reduce tension.

When he got married, Mallon and his wife smoked together. However, Mallon's wife began to experience health complications from smoking. She was diagnosed with chronic obstructive pulmonary disease, and doctors urged her to quit smoking. So, Mallon and his wife worked to quit smoking together, using nicotine patches and other cessation tools. "Giving up smoking prolonged her life and allowed us to experience 18 more years together as a married couple. My wife would have died within 10 years of her diagnosis if she hadn't quit smoking,"[6] asserts Mallon.

When Mallon's wife passed away from a heart attack, Mallon started smoking again. "I began smoking again the very day that my wife died. I had a cigarette to suppress my emotions, and I continued smoking for roughly a year," he says. Eventually, Mallon became determined to quit smoking in his wife's memory.

> "I'd encourage smokers to try a vape. Vapes work, and they are a clean source of nicotine that takes care of the cravings without the tar and other horrendous carcinogenic chemicals."[8]
>
> —Liam Mallon, a smoker who used vaping to quit

He consulted a smoking cessation coach who encouraged him to try vaping as a nicotine replacement product. By working with his coach and vaping, Mallon was able to quit smoking successfully. "Using a vape is a lot easier and a lot healthier. It's the same action of lifting your hand to your mouth, you inhale the same way, but instead of the toxic chemicals, it's a clean source of nicotine,"[7] he says.

After he quit smoking, Mallon's friends noticed a difference in his appearance. His skin looked fresher and had a healthy color. They also noticed that he no longer smelled like stale tobacco. Mallon also saved money by not buying packs of cigarettes weekly. Today, Mallon credits vaping with helping him change his life and quit smoking. "I'd encourage smokers to try a vape. Vapes work, and they are a clean source of nicotine that takes care of the cravings without the tar and other horrendous carcinogenic chemicals,"[8] he says.

An Alternative to Smoking

Many adult smokers like Liam Mallon have turned to vaping as an alternative to smoking cigarettes. The negative health impact of traditional tobacco cigarettes has been well documented. Smoking can lead to serious health conditions, including heart disease, cancer, and lung disease. According to the CDC, more than 16 million US adults have a smoking-related disease. These smoking-related conditions can negatively impact a person's quality of life and, in some cases, can even lead to death. According to the CDC, cigarette smoke causes more than 480,000 deaths annually and is the leading preventable cause of death, disease, and disability in the United States.

Quitting smoking has been proven to improve health and reduce the risk of smoking-related diseases and death. Yet quitting

Smoke shops like this one in Sterling Heights, Michigan, stock tobacco products along with vaping supplies and other smoking needs.

smoking is often very difficult. Many smokers struggle to quit because they are addicted to the nicotine in cigarettes. Nicotine is a highly addictive chemical compound. Smoking delivers nicotine into the bloodstream through the lungs. When nicotine reaches the brain, it triggers the release of feel-good chemicals. With repeated use, smokers need more nicotine to feel normal. When people try to stop smoking, their brains and bodies go through withdrawal. They might feel anxious or irritable and have trouble concentrating or sleeping. Withdrawal symptoms improve over time as the brain becomes used to not having nicotine.

Smoking cessation products can help a person quit smoking. Many cessation products use nicotine replacement therapy (NRT) to help people quit. Nicotine patches, gum, lozenges, sprays, and inhalers fall into this category. They work by replacing the nicotine in cigarettes to reduce the withdrawal symptoms a person experiences when quitting smoking. People can gradually reduce the amount of nicotine they get from these products over several weeks until their brain adjusts to not having nicotine. Without the help of a smoking cessation product, only about 5 percent of people who try to quit smoking are successful, according to the Mayo Clinic.

A New Tool

E-cigarettes have drawn a lot of interest as a new tool to help smokers quit. Similar to other NRT products, e-cigarettes provide nicotine to users without the harmful chemicals found in traditional cigarettes. E-cigarettes have different nicotine strengths; this enables users to gradually wean from their nicotine use.

E-cigarettes have several additional benefits as an alternative to smoking. Unlike smoking, vaping does not leave a lingering smell of smoke on users, and it eliminates secondhand smoke. Some people find that vaping helps to break the routine of smoking in a way that nicotine patches, gums, and lozenges do not.

Invention of the E-Cigarette

A Chinese pharmacist named Hon Lik invented the first commercially successful electronic cigarette in 2003. Lik's father was a smoker who died from lung cancer. Spurred by his father's death, Lik set out to create a smoking alternative that was healthier than cigarettes. "He wanted to develop a pure form of nicotine that could help smokers quit, but without the thousands of harmful chemicals that come from burning cigarettes," says Suchitra Krishnan-Sarin, codirector of the Yale Tobacco Center for Regulatory Science. After a bad experience with a nicotine patch, Lik came up with the idea of vaporizing nicotine in a device that simulated the actions of smoking. Lik's e-cigarette had a small battery that heated and vaporized a liquid that contained nicotine and other ingredients. Users inhaled the vapor. Lik obtained patents for his e-cigarette, which he later sold to a subsidiary of the United Kingdom's Imperial Tobacco, a multinational tobacco company. Today, most e-cigarettes still use Lik's basic design.

Quoted in Carrie Macmillan, "The Juul E-Cigarette Ban: Will It Make a Difference?," Yale Medicine, July 6, 2022. www.yalemedicine.org.

Often, smoking is part of a person's routine, something they do in certain situations. Vaping can replace cigarettes in these situations, re-creating the hand-to-mouth action of smoking. Also, vaping can produce a sensation in the throat similar to smoking.

Vaping helped thirty-year-old Allison Boughner finally quit a fifteen-year smoking habit. After being diagnosed with a blood clot in her leg, Boughner knew it was time to get serious about quitting. "My hematologist strongly advised me to quit for good, so I tried everything I could: patches, gum, and even prescription medications designed to help you stop smoking. But nothing worked. I found myself frustrated and back at square one," she concedes. Boughner finally succeeded after starting a new job. Her new employers had used e-cigarettes to quit smoking and encouraged Boughner to try vaping. The effects were immediate. "I was blown away. Without even realizing it, I was done with cigarettes. A few days into vaping, my battery died while I was out at a bar. I thought, 'Well, I'll just step outside and have a cigarette.' But when I took that first puff, the taste was awful, disgusting even. That was it. I never smoked another cigarette again,"[9] she says.

Harm Reduction Strategy

Public health officials have worked for years to reduce smoking and the health harms that come from it. Yet despite their efforts, more than 49 million US adults reported current tobacco use in 2022, according to the CDC. Many of these tobacco users are unwilling or unable to quit. For this population, some people believe that e-cigarettes can be part of a harm reduction strategy that substitutes lower-risk nicotine products for higher-risk traditional cigarettes.

> **"E-Cigarettes provide a satisfying alternative to smoking, with similar nicotine delivery, sensory stimulation, enjoyable flavors, and behavioral rituals."[10]**
>
> **—Clive D. Bates, director of Counterfactual**

A harm reduction strategy is different from attempting to stop all smoking. Often, smokers fail multiple times to quit smoking.

Some people use nicotine patches to help them quit smoking. Others find vapes, with their ability to deliver a small, measured dose of nicotine, to be a more effective alternative.

A harm reduction strategy recognizes that not all smokers will be able to quit smoking altogether. However, if they can replace some traditional cigarettes with lower-risk e-cigarettes, the overall harm to their health can be reduced. Clive D. Bates, the director of Counterfactual, a consulting and advocacy organization with a focus on public health, explains:

> E-Cigarettes provide a satisfying alternative to smoking, with similar nicotine delivery, sensory stimulation, enjoyable flavors, and behavioral rituals. For many users, they are pleasurable and fun, and there is a subculture associated with their use. By asking smokers to give up less of the smoking experience, switching to e-cigarettes can be a more effective replacement for smoking.[10]

Emerging Research

Research on the effectiveness of e-cigarettes as a smoking cessation tool is still emerging. Some early research suggests that e-

Vaping Versus Medication

Varenicline is a prescription medication that is considered one of the most effective smoking cessation tools available. Unlike many smoking cessation tools, varenicline does not contain nicotine. It works by blocking nicotine's effects on the brain. It blocks the good feeling that nicotine produces, which makes smoking less enjoyable. The medication also can help prevent cravings to smoke cigarettes and reduce withdrawal symptoms. However, varenicline can have side effects, such as vivid dreams and insomnia. New research suggests that vaping may be just as effective as varenicline to help people stop smoking. In a 2024 study published in *JAMA Internal Medicine*, a clinical trial that compared participants using varenicline and e-cigarettes as smoking cessation tools had approximately equal success rates. "Varenicline's long track record of efficacy and safety and its approval from FDA [the US Food and Drug Administration] as a smoking cessation aid favors it as the first-line choice, but this study indicates that [e-cigarettes] are certainly an option for people who are unsuccessful with or cannot tolerate varenicline," says Nancy Rigotti, director of the Tobacco Research and Treatment Center at Massachusetts General Hospital.

Quoted in Nicholas Florko, "Vaping Is Just as Good as Chantix at Helping People Quit Cigarettes, New Study Finds," *STAT*, June 17, 2024. www.statnews.com.

cigarettes can be an effective tool to help people stop smoking. A 2023 study from the Hollings Cancer Center at the Medical University of South Carolina (MUSC) found that using e-cigarettes helped study participants quit smoking, even if they did not intend to quit when the study began. The study, the largest trial of e-cigarettes today in the United States, attempted to re-create real-world conditions. Participants were divided into two groups and followed over four years. Smokers in the first group were given e-cigarettes and told they could decide whether or not to use them, as much or as little as they wanted; smokers in the second group did not receive e-cigarettes. Researchers found that participants in the e-cigarette group were more likely to quit smoking entirely or reduce the number of cigarettes smoked each day than those in the control group. "No matter how we looked at it, those who got the e-cigarette product demonstrated greater abstinence and reduced harm as compared to those who didn't get it,"[11] states Matthew Carpenter, codirector of the Tobacco Research Program at the MUSC Hollings Cancer Center.

Other studies have had similar results. In a 2023 study published in the journal *Nature Medicine*, researchers from several universities reviewed numerous studies and clinical trials on the use of e-cigarettes as a smoking cessation tool. The researchers found consistent evidence that adult smokers who vaped frequently were significantly more likely to quit smoking than smokers who did not vape. According to the study's authors,

> Vaping of most newer-generation e-cigarettes results in the delivery of nicotine to the lungs in a manner similar to that of cigarettes. These e-cigarettes pose a risk of nicotine addiction for some young people, but for adults already addicted to cigarettes—the single deadliest consumer product ever invented—they also serve as an important, less-hazardous alternative to continued smoking.[12]

Yet other research has been inconclusive on the effectiveness of e-cigarettes to help people stop smoking. In 2020, researchers at the University of California, San Diego (UCSD) published the results of two analyses of data from the Population Assessment of Tobacco and Health Study, which studies tobacco use and its effects on health in the United States. Both analyses found that e-cigarettes did not help smokers quit tobacco use. One analysis published in September 2020 in the journal *PLOS ONE* followed 2,770 smokers who reported they were trying to quit smoking. At a one-year follow-up, the percentage of participants who were successful at quitting showed little difference among participants who used e-cigarettes, those who used a different smoking cessation tool, and those who used neither. "Among this representa-

Research on the effectiveness of vapes as a smoking cessation tool is still emerging. Some studies support the notion that vapes help people to quit cigarettes, but others do not.

tive sample of U.S. smokers trying to quit, we found no evidence that e-cigarettes were helpful in the quit attempt. This lack of effectiveness was also apparent in the sub-sample who used e-cigarettes on a daily basis for this quit attempt,"[13] contends John P. Pierce, one of the study's authors and a professor at UCSD's Moores Cancer Center.

UCSD researchers came to a similar conclusion in a second analysis published in July 2020. They found no evidence that smokers who used e-cigarettes to quit smoking did not have significantly different success rates than smokers who did not use e-cigarettes. They did, however, find that participants who used e-cigarettes to help quit smoking were more likely to be using nicotine at a one-year follow-up than those who did not use e-cigarettes. Karen Messer, the study's author and the director of biostatics at Moores Cancer Center, explains the findings:

> In these analyses, we carefully matched each smoker who used e-cigarettes as a cessation aid with up to two similar smokers who tried to quit without using e-cigarettes. Our results suggest that these smokers would have been just as successful in quitting smoking without the use of e-cigarettes. However, without the use of e-cigarettes, they would have been more successful in breaking their nicotine dependence.[14]

Two Habits

Although some people have had success using e-cigarettes to stop smoking, many continue vaping long after they quit smoking. Also, those who fail to stop smoking often find themselves with two habits: smoking and vaping, which increases potential health risks. "One of the best things you can do for your health is to stop smoking. While e-cigarettes may work for some people, they're hindering quit attempts for other people,"[15] warns Amanda Palmer, a postdoctoral fellow in MUSC's Department of Public Health Sciences.

"E-cigarettes are addictive and are not 100% safe. If you're considering vaping as a method to quit smoking, consider some of the risks and benefits, and be aware that many people continue to vape after they quit smoking."[16]

—Amanda Palmer, a postdoctoral fellow at the Medical University of South Carolina

Until more research is completed on the long-term effects and effectiveness of e-cigarettes as a smoking cessation tool, Palmer recommends that people think carefully about whether to use them to stop smoking. "E-cigarettes are addictive and are not 100% safe. If you're considering vaping as a method to quit smoking, consider some of the risks and benefits, and be aware that many people continue to vape after they quit smoking,"[16] says Palmer. A person may simply be trading one harmful practice for another.

CHAPTER TWO

Nicotine Addiction

Belle Moore, a teen from Lancashire, England, started vaping at age sixteen. Some of her friends vaped and persuaded Moore to try e-cigarettes. Now, at age nineteen, Moore is addicted to vaping and feels the need to vape every few hours. "I start to get shaky, and it's almost all I can think of," she says. Moore has tried to quit vaping twice but has been unsuccessful. Today, she feels as if vaping is taking over her life, and she has also started smoking cigarettes. "It honestly feels like I have no control over it,"[17] she admits. Every week, a good amount of her money goes to buying vapes and cigarettes to feed her nicotine addiction. And Moore has noticed that she coughs more and gets sick more frequently.

> **"I know how much of a struggle it's been for me. . . . If there's anyone who is thinking of starting vaping or starting smoking, if they're younger, don't because it can honestly just ruin your life."[18]**
>
> —Belle Moore, a teen addicted to nicotine

Today, Moore warns young people not to start vaping. "I know how much of a struggle it's been for me. . . . If there's anyone who is thinking of starting vaping or starting smoking, if they're younger, don't because it can honestly just ruin your life,"[18] she advises.

Nicotine: A Chemical Compound

Almost all e-cigarettes contain nicotine. Nicotine is a highly addictive chemical compound. It occurs naturally in the tobacco plant, but laboratories can produce synthetic nicotine. Tobacco products such as cigarettes, chewing tobacco, and cigars also contain nicotine. Nicotine is what gives people a pleasurable buzz when they smoke or vape. It is also what drives people to keep smoking or vaping once they start. The more a person smokes or vapes, the faster the body and brain depend on nicotine to feel good, and the more difficult it becomes to stop.

Nicotine enters the body when a person inhales cigarette smoke or vape vapor into the lungs. Once nicotine reaches the lungs, it is absorbed into the bloodstream. From there, nicotine travels through the bloodstream to the brain. Nicotine causes the brain to release a neurotransmitter called dopamine. Dopamine has a role in many bodily functions, including movement, memory, attention, mood, and learning. Dopamine acts as a chemical messenger, sending messages between brain cells and between the brain and body.

Dopamine is also essential in the body's reward system, which rewards and motivates people for behaviors that will help them survive, such as eating, drinking, and reproducing. Dopamine, also known as the "feel-good" chemical, creates pleasurable feelings. When a person does something that triggers the reward system, the brain releases a large amount of dopamine. The person feels pleasure and is motivated to seek more pleasurable feelings.

Nicotine triggers the brain to release dopamine, which causes a person to experience a pleasurable buzz or feeling. The pleasurable feelings do not last long, and that leads a person to use nicotine again and again to produce the same pleasure. Over time, the body becomes dependent on nicotine and needs increasing amounts to feel good.

Elijah Stone first experimented with e-cigarettes at age nineteen. The college freshman was dealing with depression and looking for a quick way to feel better. He became hooked quickly. "The moment I felt that buzz, how was I supposed to go back after I felt that?"[19] asks Stone, who is now twenty-three and still vaping.

How Nicotine Impacts the Brain

Over time, repeated exposure to nicotine can cause changes in the brain. Some changes impact cognitive functions, including

The chemical nicotine occurs naturally in the tobacco plant, but it can also be produced synthetically. It causes the "buzz" that smokers feel after inhaling smoke or vapor.

concentration and memory. Two 2020 studies from the University of Rochester Medical Center (URMC) found evidence that vaping is linked to impaired cognitive abilities. In one study, researchers analyzed responses from a phone survey of more than 886,000 US adults. In the second study, researchers analyzed responses from more than 18,000 high school and middle school students in the National Youth Tobacco Survey. Both surveys asked similar questions about smoking and vaping habits and cognitive function.

Researchers found that in both studies, participants who smoked or vaped were more likely to report difficulty with cognitive functions. Regardless of age, those who used nicotine were more likely to have trouble concentrating, remembering, or making decisions as compared to participants who did not smoke or vape. In both studies, participants who smoked and vaped fared the worst and were the most likely to report cognitive difficulties. Participants who only used nicotine in one way—either vaping or smoking—experienced similar rates of cognitive difficulties. They were still significantly more likely to report cognitive difficulty than people who did not smoke or vape at all. "Our studies add to growing evidence that vaping should not be considered a safe alternative to tobacco smoking,"[20] insists Dongmei Li, the study's author and an associate professor at URMC. According to Li, more studies are needed to further understand the connection between vaping and cognitive difficulties.

"Our studies add to growing evidence that vaping should not be considered a safe alternative to tobacco smoking."[20]

—Dongmei Li, an associate professor at the University of Rochester Medical Center

Nicotine also affects the brain's reward processes that motivate positive behaviors and the executive function that controls and manages thoughts, actions, and emotions. Francesco Versace, a professor at the University of Texas MD Anderson Cancer Center, explains:

> When nicotine hits the brain, it produces effects that are similar to those produced by other rewards like food, sex, and social connection. Nicotine can "hijack" the brain mechanisms that support reward and executive functions and bias them toward nicotine and nicotine-associated cues. This means that through repeated exposures, the brain learns that certain cues, such as vape logos and even the shape of a vape device, are associated with nicotine. The associations between these cues and nicotine can be so strong that they lead to addiction.[21]

Nicotine affects each person's brain differently, which can influence who may develop a nicotine addiction and who does not. As Versace points out,

> there are large individual differences in the effects of nicotine on the brain. Some individuals have stronger brain responses to these nicotine-related cues than to non-drug-related rewards. For them, resisting the lure of nicotine is more difficult. These individuals tend to compulsively use nicotine when exposed to nicotine-related cues. They are also more likely to relapse when they try to quit.[22]

Nicotine and Mental Health

Nicotine can also affect a person's mental health. People who struggle with nicotine addiction often have a higher risk of developing other behavioral and mental health conditions. These include attention-deficit hyperactivity disorder (ADHD), depression and anxiety disorders, and other substance use disorders. Some people with mental health conditions use nicotine to self-medicate and relieve their mental health symptoms. However, using nicotine to relieve mental health symptoms can become a vicious cycle where they need increasing amounts of nicotine to feel normal. Over time, nicotine addiction can worsen mental health symptoms.

A 2024 study from researchers at the University of Surrey in England investigated the relationship between vaping, anxiety, and sleep quality in young adults aged eighteen to twenty-five. They conducted a survey asking participants about their vaping habits, mental health, and sleep quality. Researchers found that participants who vaped reported significantly higher levels of anxiety symptoms. Additionally, the vaping group also report-

Nicotine Poisoning

Nicotine poisoning can occur when a person has too much nicotine in the body. Before e-cigarettes, nicotine poisoning was rare. Most cases occurred when someone accidentally consumed tobacco or nicotine-containing plants. However, nicotine poisoning has become more common in recent years because of e-cigarettes and the liquid products they use. The concentration of nicotine in vape pods and other e-liquids is higher than in past tobacco cigarettes and products. Nicotine poisoning can affect anyone, but children are at increased risk because of their smaller size and weight. Nicotine can enter the body by being inhaled through smoking and vaping or absorbed through the membranes of the mouth or intestines. The skin can even absorb liquid nicotine if it is spilled or touched. Symptoms of nicotine poisoning include nausea and vomiting, stomachache, increased heart rate and blood pressure, headache, watery mouth, increased breathing, dizziness and tremors, confusion, and anxiety. In some severe cases, nicotine poisoning can lead to muscle paralysis, coma, and death.

When the nicotine in e-cigarette vapor hits the brain's "reward centers," it produces a wave of good feelings that make the user want more.

ed poorer sleep quality, with more than 75 percent experiencing symptoms of insomnia. "In this study, we found a disturbing link between vape use and anxiety symptoms, and it can become a vicious cycle of using a vape to soothe anxiety but then being unable to sleep, making you feel worse in the long run,"[23] explains Simon Evans, a lecturer at the University of Surrey.

The Surrey study also found that participants who vaped reported higher alcohol use. Evans says,

> It is now common to see a young person vaping. . . . What is worrying is that many are unaware of or simply downplay the dangers of such products, believing that something that tastes "fruity" could not be harmful. This is not the case as the nicotine contained in the products is known to negatively affect brain development and may induce behaviors that increase the risk of developing substance abuse issues.[24]

Increased Nicotine Levels

The risks of nicotine may be more significant with e-cigarettes. The concentration of nicotine in vapes can be much higher than in traditional cigarettes, increasing the health and addiction risks. On average, a traditional cigarette has about 10 to 12 milligrams (mg) of nicotine. However, not every milligram of nicotine is inhaled during smoking, and only about 1.2 to 1.8 mg enter the body with each cigarette. For a standard pack of twenty cigarettes, the average smoker inhales about 24 to 36 mg of nicotine. In comparison, e-cigarettes come in different nicotine strengths; on average, the nicotine in e-cigarettes ranges from 0.5 mg to 15.4 mg per fifteen puffs.

In recent years, the nicotine content of e-cigarettes sold in the United States has grown. A 2023 study of nicotine strength among e-cigarette products found that the average nicotine concentration in e-cigarettes increased from 2.5 percent to 4.4 percent between 2017 and 2022, a 76 percent increase in strength. As nicotine increases in e-cigarettes, many health experts are concerned about the negative effects it will have on health and addiction. They warn that users, especially young people, may become addicted to the nicotine in e-cigarettes within days. "We've never

Behavioral Support

For those addicted to nicotine, behavioral support and counseling can be an essential part of overcoming the addiction. Addiction specialists typically provide behavioral counseling for nicotine addiction over several sessions. Counseling can occur in individual or group settings. Often, behavioral counseling combined with medication is the most effective approach to treat nicotine addiction. Some counselors use cognitive behavioral therapy to help patients identify the people and environments that trigger nicotine cravings and learn coping strategies to stop nicotine use. Other counselors use mindfulness-based treatments to help patients become aware of the sensations, cravings, and thoughts that trigger cravings for nicotine and learn techniques to handle them without turning to nicotine. Online technologies such as cell phone apps, internet sites, and social media platforms also provide interventions to support those who struggle with nicotine addiction.

E-cigarette manufacturers believe vapes are better for users than combustible forms of smoking, like cigarettes and cigars.

delivered this level of nicotine before. We really don't know the long-term health implications,"[25] states Matthew Myers, president of the Campaign for Tobacco-Free Kids.

The e-cigarette industry acknowledges that the nicotine in e-cigarettes is addictive, but it emphasizes that it can be used in a positive way to improve the health of smokers. Strong nicotine concentrations in vaping products can be more effective in helping adult smokers quit tobacco products and replace them with e-cigarettes, which are overall less harmful to health. "The goal is to get people away from combustible products," says Nicholas Minas Alfaro, chief executive officer of Puff Bar, an e-cigarette brand. Still, Alfaro admits that "these products are addictive products; there's no hiding that."[26]

Nicotine Addiction

As many smokers know, overcoming a nicotine addiction is no easy task. Nicotine is one of the most addictive substances worldwide.

A person who vapes can quickly develop a nicotine addiction. The more a person vapes, the more the brain and body learn to rely on nicotine to feel good. Before long, the brain and body need increasing amounts of nicotine to simply function normally.

People who have become addicted to nicotine find that even when they try to quit, they cannot give it up. They experience withdrawal symptoms when they try to stop using nicotine. Physically, they may experience cravings, restlessness, difficulty concentrating, increased hunger, sleep difficulties, and gastrointestinal problems. Emotionally, they may find themselves becoming increasingly irritable, anxious, or depressed. They may have trouble concentrating and feel frustrated or angry. Those addicted to nicotine will continue to use it even if they have health problems related to vaping. And they may even choose to avoid social situations where they cannot vape.

Nicotine's powerful addiction is what makes it so hard for people to quit. Fourteen-year-old Liam knows firsthand how difficult it is to stop vaping. The teen from West Yorkshire, England, started vaping at age thirteen with friends. At first, he hid his vaping habit from his mother, Sarah, but she later caught him vaping in his room. A year later, Liam vapes daily, on the way to school, between classes, and on the way home. He tried to quit once, but he did not last a day without vaping. "He was just beside himself with craving. He just couldn't calm down—he was saying: 'I'm never going to be able to stop.' It broke my heart,"[27] says Sarah. Liam's addiction interferes with activities that he used to enjoy. He used to love mountain biking, but now he gets winded too quickly.

E-cigarettes may contain fewer harmful chemicals than traditional cigarettes. Yet they are not without risk. Most e-cigarettes have higher levels of nicotine than traditional cigarettes. Repeated exposure to nicotine can lead to potential brain, health, and addiction problems.

CHAPTER THREE

The Impact on Health

Ryan first experimented with vaping in college. At parties, he noticed classmates using e-cigarettes, and several of his friends had started vaping. Ryan heard that vaping was healthier than smoking cigarettes, and no one he knew had experienced any health problems from vaping. He was not worried about his health when he tried his first e-cigarette.

Before long, Ryan was addicted to vaping. He vaped throughout the day, and it was much easier to hide than smoking cigarettes. What he did not know, however, was that his constant vaping was damaging his lungs. "It's very hard to know the damage you are doing to your lungs because you don't see them every day. It's not like a cut or something. And though you may feel small changes over time, they are easy to ignore or write off as a cold,"[28] he says.

One day, Ryan went to the doctor for medicine to treat a routine upper respiratory infection. However, he did not feel better on the medication, and he soon began to feel worse. When he became short of breath, Ryan went to the emergency room, where doctors x-rayed his chest. The X-ray appeared clear, so doctors sent Ryan home. Two days later, Ryan's health took a dramatic turn for the worse, and he struggled to breathe. An ambulance rushed him to the hospital, where tests showed that his blood oxygen levels had dropped to 85 percent, well below normal levels of 95 percent or higher. Ryan's breathing rate and heart rate had also soared as he struggled to get enough oxygen to support his body. He was in critical condition.

Doctors immediately intubated Ryan and put him on a ventilator to help him breathe. "At that point, they didn't know what the problem was because he was so sick when they intubated him that they could not take a sample from his lungs. So, for those first few days, he was on 16 machines, and they were giving him every antibiotic, steroids, and anti-inflammatory they could because they had no idea what was wrong,"[29] Ryan's parents explain.

After doctors were finally able to biopsy Ryan's lungs, they diagnosed him with staphylococcal pneumonia, a bacterial lung infection. They explained that because Ryan's health had worsened so quickly, they believed his condition was caused by vaping. Ryan had vaped while he had a cold, a typical upper respiratory infection. Ryan did not know that vaping while having a bacterial infection can cause the bacteria to grow and spread rapidly. In Ryan's case, doctors believed that vaping caused the bacteria to spread inside Ryan's body. Blood clots formed in his legs. When the blood clots broke off and traveled via the bloodstream to his lungs, Ryan's lungs failed.

"I tell people to just stay away from vaping. It's very addictive, and if you keep doing it, it gets to the point where there will be something bad that happens to you."[30]

—Ryan, a young adult hospitalized after vaping

After several weeks in the hospital, Ryan finally went home. At first, he was so weak he had to use a wheelchair. At physical therapy, Ryan regained the strength to stand and walk. Today, he continues to improve by following a healthy lifestyle that does not include vaping. "You really take breathing for granted, and you don't realize how much you will miss it until you can't do it," Ryan says. Many of his family members and friends have also quit vaping after seeing what it did to his health. He adds, "I tell people to just stay away from vaping. It's very addictive, and if you keep doing it, it gets to the point where there will be something bad that happens to you. I wish that I had been able to have the discipline to stay away from things that my friends and family had told me were dangerous."[30]

Safe or Not?

Vaping is often marketed as a safer alternative to smoking traditional cigarettes. In some ways, this is true. Years of research have shown how smoking significantly harms health. Smoking damages every body organ. It is responsible for more than 480,000 US deaths annually, according to the CDC. Tobacco smoke contains thousands of chemicals, including toxins such as nicotine, carbon monoxide, tar, benzene, arsenic, and formaldehyde. Every time smokers inhale, they draw these chemicals into their bodies and increase their risk of heart disease, cancer, and lung disease.

E-cigarettes do not contain many of the harmful chemicals in traditional cigarettes. However, that does not mean vaping is entirely safe. There are still several chemicals and potentially harmful ingredients in e-cigarettes. These substances enter the body every time a person inhales e-cigarette vapor. Research on the health effects of vaping is still in the early stages; however, some studies suggest that vaping can be harmful to health.

There is a proven link between cigarette smoking and negative health outcomes. Vaping delivers fewer harmful chemicals, but may still affect long-term health.

Fires and Explosions

E-cigarettes can cause injury beyond heart and lung damage and addiction. E-cigarettes use a rechargeable lithium-ion battery to heat e-liquid and turn it into vapor. Some defective e-cigarette batteries have caused fires and explosions. Many times, the e-cigarette battery explodes while in a user's pocket, sending small shrapnel-like particles into nearby tissue and causing burn injuries to the legs, groin, and hand. If the device is near a user's face, the explosion can cause injury and burns to the face and eyes. There have been cases where the battery exploded with enough force to break the user's jaw. Shannon Acker, a pediatric surgeon at Children's Hospital Colorado, participated in a 2022 research study on the potential for e-cigarettes to explode during use. The study reviewed the cases of fifteen youths who were injured from exploding e-cigarettes. Ten of the fifteen patients were hospitalized, with three needing intensive care. According to Acker, nearly half of the patients required surgery for their injuries, including skin grafts, broken bone repairs, and dental surgery.

Cardiovascular Disease

Some research suggests that vaping increases a person's risk of cardiovascular disease. For example, one large study found that people who vaped were 34 percent more likely to have a heart attack as compared to people who did not smoke or vape. The vapers were also 25 percent more likely to develop heart disease. Scientists suspect that the nicotine in e-cigarettes may be one of the causes. "Nicotine increases your heart rate and blood pressure. It can also constrict blood vessels, leading to decreased blood supply to organs throughout your body, resulting in an increased risk for heart attacks, strokes, and abnormal—sometimes fatal—heart rhythms, such as atrial fibrillation and ventricular fibrillation,"[31] explains cardiologist Michel Corban.

For years, scientists have known that smoking increases a person's risk of cardiovascular disease by damaging the body's blood vessels. Some chemicals in e-cigarette vapor may also damage the membranes that line all blood vessels. "When this occurs, it can put you at greater risk for developing atherosclerosis, sometimes called hardening of the arteries, and heart attacks,"[32] comments Corban.

New research, funded by the National Institutes of Health (NIH) and published in 2022, shows that vaping also may cause damage to blood vessels and increase the risk of cardiovascular disease. In one study, researchers at the University of California, San Francisco (UCSF) collected blood samples from participants who were either long-term smokers, long-term vapers, or did not use either type of cigarette. They tested the blood samples to determine the health and function of the participants' blood vessels. They noted several indications of damage to the long-term vaping group's blood vessels. For example, researchers found that the long-term vaping group had more permeable blood cells than either the smoker or nonuser groups. Too much permeability in blood cells can lead to leaky blood vessels. "We found that chronic e-cigarette users had impaired blood vessel function, which may put them at increased risk for heart disease. It indicates that chronic users of e-cigarettes may experience a risk of vascular disease similar to that of chronic smokers,"[33] says Matthew Springer, the study's leader and a professor at UCSF.

> **"We found that chronic e-cigarette users had impaired blood vessel function, which may put them at increased risk for heart disease."[33]**
>
> **—Matthew Springer, a professor at the University of California, San Francisco**

Vaping may damage the cardiovascular system differently than smoking tobacco. In their research, Springer and his team studied cardiac biomarkers. When the heart is stressed or damaged, the body releases substances called cardiac biomarkers into the blood. Cardiac biomarkers can be enzymes, hormones, or proteins. Doctors use cardiac biomarkers to help diagnose, determine risk, and manage cardiovascular disease. When examining the participants' blood samples, researchers found that smokers and vapers both had high levels of cardiac biomarkers in their blood, but the specific biomarkers were different. "These findings suggest that using the two products together, as many people do, could increase their health risks compared to using them individually. We had not expected to see that,"[34] notes Springer.

In a second study, Springer's research team investigated whether specific chemicals in cigarette smoke or e-cigarette vapor caused blood vessel damage. In studies using lab rats, the researchers tested the animals with substances found in either tobacco smoke or e-cigarette vapor. They also tested specific nanoparticles to represent the particles in smoke and vapor. The team found that no specific component of either cigarette smoke or e-cigarette vapor caused blood vessel damage. Instead, they suspect airway irritation caused by smoking or vaping may be the root cause of damage. Researchers suspect that airway irritation may trigger a response, possibly an inflammatory response, that causes damage to blood vessels. "We were surprised to find that there was not a single component that you could remove to stop the damaging effect of smoke or vapors on the blood vessels. As long as there's an irritant in the airway, blood vessel function may be impaired,"[35] Springer explains.

Research on lab rats suggests that despite their different chemical content, both cigarette smoke and e-cigarette vapor irritate and damage blood vessels.

Vaping may also increase the user's risk of heart failure, a condition in which the heart muscle is damaged and cannot pump enough blood for the body. A study by researchers at MedStar Health in Baltimore found that people who used e-cigarettes at any point in their lives were 19 percent more likely to experience heart failure than those who had never vaped. For the study, researchers reviewed and analyzed data from more than 175,000 US adults collected by the NIH. Study author Yakubu Bene-Alhasan, a resident physician at MedStar Health, believes that more research is needed on the effects of vaping on heart health and heart failure. However, he says doctors should warn patients about the potential risk of heart failure from vaping: "Although more research is required, patients still need to know what we know about it now so they can make informed decisions."[36]

Damage to Lungs

E-cigarettes contain fewer chemicals and toxins than tobacco cigarettes, but that does not mean they are safe. E-cigarettes heat a liquid called vape juice or e-liquid until it becomes a vapor. E-liquid contains flavorings, additives, nicotine, and other chemicals that travel into the lungs with inhaled vapor. "Most e-cigarettes contain freebase nicotine or nicotine salts, some contain vitamin E acetate, and many produce a vapor containing a number of harmful chemicals including diacetyl, formaldehyde, acrolein, benzene, other toxicants, carcinogens, and heavy metals,"[37] notes Corban.

One potential damaging substance in e-cigarette vapor is vitamin E acetate, which is often used as a thickening agent in e-liquid. Typically, vitamin E acetate is safely used in hair and skin products. However, when inhaled in e-cigarette vapor, vitamin E acetate may be unsafe. Doctors have found that people with significant vaping lung damage often have vitamin E acetate present in their lungs. "We think that some of the vaporized elements of

> "We think that some of the vaporized elements of the oil are getting deep down into the lungs and causing an inflammatory response."[38]
>
> —Stephen R. Broderick, a professor of surgery at Johns Hopkins University School of Medicine

the oil are getting deep down into the lungs and causing an inflammatory response,"[38] says Stephen R. Broderick, a professor of surgery at the Johns Hopkins University School of Medicine. In response to these findings, the CDC has identified vitamin E acetate as a chemical of concern, meaning it can potentially cause significant health risks and further study is needed.

Other potentially harmful substances commonly found in e-liquid or produced when the liquid is heated include diacetyl, formaldehyde, and acrolein. Diacetyl is a food additive often added to e-liquids to make them taste better. Inhaling this chemical causes lung inflammation and can lead to permanent scarring in the airways of lungs, making it harder to breathe. Formaldehyde has been linked to lung and heart disease, and acrolein, frequently used as a weed killer, has also been linked to lung damage.

In 2019, the first long-term study on vaping and lung health found that vaping significantly increased a person's risk of developing chronic lung diseases such as asthma, bronchitis, emphysema, and chronic obstructive pulmonary disease. In the study, researchers followed thirty-two thousand adults for several years. Initially, none of the participants had any sign of lung disease. Within three years, researchers found that participants who vaped were 30 percent more likely to have developed a chronic lung disease as compared to nonvapers. "E-cigarette use predicted the development of lung disease over a very short period of time. It only took three years,"[39] states Stanton Glantz, the study's author and a professor at UCSF.

In a 2023 study, investigators from Ohio State University and the University of Southern California's Keck School of Medicine found that vaping increased respiratory symptoms in young adults. Researchers followed a group of more than two thousand

A 2019 study found that vaping significantly increased a person's chance of developing chronic lung diseases such as asthma, bronchitis, emphysema, and chronic obstructive pulmonary disease.

US teens across four years and surveyed participants annually about their vaping habits and respiratory symptoms. Teens who vaped during the past thirty days were 81 percent more likely to report wheezing and 78 percent more likely to report shortness of breath than those who did not vape. Vaping teens were also twice as likely to experience bronchitis symptoms as compared to non-users. "This study contributes to emerging evidence from human and toxicological studies that e-cigarette use is associated with increased risk for developing respiratory symptoms, and it should be considered in the regulation of e-cigarettes to minimize the health impact of e-cigarette product use among young people,"[40] comments Alayna Tackett, a researcher at Ohio State University.

EVALI

In mid-2019, the CDC started investigating a dramatic rise in hospitalizations related to vaping. Patients presented various respiratory symptoms, such as shortness of breath, coughing,

Oral Health

The chemicals in e-cigarettes can damage the tissues in the mouth and gums. Nicotine decreases blood flow to the gums, which can increase the risk of periodontal or gum disease. Gum disease affects the gums and tissues that support teeth. Gums may become red, tender, and swollen. They may bleed easily and recede. Gum disease that progresses may lead to tooth infection and loss. Other chemicals in e-cigarettes, such as propylene glycol, benzene, and formaldehyde, increase the risk of gum disease. A 2020 study found that 43 percent of people who vaped had gum disease and oral infections as compared to 28 percent of people who did not vape or smoke. "Periodontal disease is normally an adult disease, and we're seeing it in younger people. Younger people normally have more saliva than they need, so when they present with dry mouth, periodontal disease, or increased complaints of mouth ulcers, our next question is, 'Do you vape?' These symptoms are all tied to components in e-cigarettes," explains Crystal Stinson, an assistant professor at Texas A&M College of Dentistry. Stinson has also noticed more cavities in patients who vape. She suspects that e-liquid may have acidic components that damage the protective enamel on teeth.

Michael Precker, "Need Another Reason Not to Vape? Your Oral Health Is at Risk," American Heart Association, August 26, 2020. www.heart.org.

and chest pain. All admitted to vaping within the previous three months. Doctors began calling these lung cases "e-cigarette or vaping product use-associated lung injury" or EVALI.

EVALI is a serious and potentially fatal condition that causes severe inflammation in the lungs. People with EVALI often experience shortness of breath, coughing, rapid breathing, chest pain, fever and chills, gastrointestinal distress, and rapid heart rate. Scientists believe that the vitamin E acetate and other chemicals in vaping vapor cause EVALI, but more research is needed. X-rays or scans of the lungs may show areas of tissue damage.

Almost all patients with EVALI need to be hospitalized. Treatment depends on the symptoms and includes antibiotics to fight infection and corticosteroids to reduce lung inflammation. Sometimes, patients may be given supplemental oxygen or placed on a ventilator if they cannot breathe independently. Because the illness is so new, scientists are unsure about the long-term recovery and prognosis of EVALI patients. “At its core, EVALI is a serious disease that primarily affects the lungs and results in a substantial number of hospitalizations and deaths in a relatively young and otherwise healthy population across the United States,” notes Meghan Rebuli, an assistant professor at the University of North Carolina School of Medicine. “This epidemic is largely caused by the unregulated and quickly evolving nature of the e-cigarette industry and certainly highlights the need for continued action by both researchers and government agencies.”[41]

E-cigarettes contain fewer harmful chemicals than traditional cigarettes. Yet there is a growing body of research that indicates vaping can cause long-term health consequences, from heart disease to lasting lung damage. More research is needed to understand these risks better. Meanwhile, medical professionals urge people who are considering vaping to be cautious and consider the potential impact on their health.

CHAPTER FOUR

Youth and Vaping

Ruby Ellis first picked up an e-cigarette when she was fourteen years old. Most of her friends and classmates also vaped. The young Australian teen had no problems getting e-cigarettes even though it was illegal to sell them to people under age eighteen. She quickly became addicted to vaping. At the peak of her addiction, Ellis estimates that she took about three thousand puffs weekly and hid a stash of about seven vape pens in a drawer in her bedroom. "It seriously becomes an issue when it's the first thing you think of when you wake up in the morning. You wake up and go 'where is it? where is my vape?' and it's the last thing you do before you go to bed. You know, like, 'I'll just have one more hit of the vape,'"[42] she says.

Ellis's addiction began to take a physical toll on her. "I would pass out a lot. I would be super light-headed, super dizzy. I'd be on the floor in a minute, you know, complete loss of consciousness,"[43] she recalls. Sometimes, she would shake until she could take a puff of her vape. The addiction also drove her to search through the trash for a vape without hesitation when she needed a puff.

For a while, Ellis hid her vaping addiction from her parents. Even if they were in the same room, she would quickly sneak a puff from her vape pen when they turned their backs. When her mother noticed her physical shaking, Ellis explained it away. Her mother notes, "We're looking out for the usual things you look out for with your kids, so we're looking out for cigarette smells, looking for changes in behavior in case [they are] drug affected, if there's any alcohol, but with vapes, there's literally no sign at all."[44] Eventually, Ellis talked to her mother about her vaping addiction. Now, she is grateful that her parents support her efforts to overcome the addiction.

A New Habit

Since their introduction in the United States around 2007, e-cigarettes have become very popular with teens and young adults. Among US middle and high school students, e-cigarettes were the most commonly used tobacco product in 2024, according to data from the 2024 National Youth Tobacco Survey and the CDC. The survey reports that 1.63 million (5.9 percent) of middle and high school students currently use vaping products. That number was good news for some officials because it was the lowest in a decade. "The continued decline in e-cigarette use among our nation's youth is a monumental public health win. This progress is a testament to the relentless efforts by the FDA [US Food and Drug Administration], CDC, and others, particularly over the past half-decade. But we can't rest on our laurels, as there's still more work to do to further reduce youth e-cigarette use,"[45] says Brian King, director of the FDA's Center for Tobacco Products.

> **"Youth use of tobacco products in any form—including e-cigarettes and nicotine pouches—is unsafe."[46]**
>
> **—Deirdre Lawrence Kittner, director of the CDC's Office on Smoking and Health**

Although youth e-cigarette use has declined, many people recognize that it is still a concern. Youth e-cigarette use is more than harmless experimentation. Many are vaping regularly, which is a sign they have already developed a nicotine dependence. According to the 2024 National Youth Tobacco Survey, more than 25 percent of young users vaped daily. Nearly 40 percent vaped during twenty of the last thirty days. "Youth use of tobacco products in any form—including e-cigarettes and nicotine pouches—is unsafe. It's essential that we remain vigilant and committed to public health efforts to ensure all youth can live healthy, tobacco-free lives,"[46] warns Deirdre Lawrence Kittner, director of the CDC's Office on Smoking and Health.

E-cigarettes are the most commonly used tobacco products among US middle and high school students. Nearly 6 percent report using vapes.

Also concerning, teens who have never smoked are picking up e-cigarettes. Some believe that e-cigarettes are healthier and cleaner than smoking. For others, e-cigarettes are generally less expensive than traditional cigarettes. "What I find most concerning about the rise of vaping is that people who would've never smoked otherwise, especially youth, are taking up the habit. It's one thing if you convert from cigarette smoking to vaping. It's quite another thing to start up nicotine use with vaping. And, getting hooked on nicotine often leads to using traditional tobacco products down the road,"[47] comments Michael Blaha, director of clinical research at the Johns Hopkins Ciccarone Center for the Prevention of Heart Disease.

Why Teens Vape

The decision to vape is an individual choice, but several factors play a role in influencing teens to start and keep vaping. Having a friend who vapes is the most common reason US teens decide to try e-cigarettes. They are curious to try vaping because they see friends and family members who use them. Often, teens get their first e-cigarettes from someone they know. Approximately 32 percent of young people get e-cigarettes from a friend, and 29 percent had someone they know buy vaping products for them, according to the CDC. Another 31 percent purchased vaping products themselves.

> "What I find most concerning about the rise of vaping is that people who would've never smoked otherwise, especially youth, are taking up the habit. It's one thing if you convert from cigarette smoking to vaping. It's quite another thing to start up nicotine use with vaping."[47]
>
> —Michael Blaha, director of clinical research at the Johns Hopkins Ciccarone Center for the Prevention of Heart Disease

E-cigarette marketing and advertising also tempt some teens to try vaping. In 2021, 70 percent of middle and high school students reported they had seen e-cigarette marketing. They saw ads on the internet, television, and streaming services as well as in movies, magazines, and newspapers. Nearly 75 percent of students also saw e-cigarette posts or content on social media sites.

Most teens who vape start with a flavored product—that is, an e-liquid that contains nicotine and a flavoring as well as other substances. In 2023, according to the CDC, approximately 90 percent of teens who vaped reported they used flavored products. Among teen users, flavors such as fruit, candy, mint, and menthol were most popular. Recognizing the appeal of flavored vaping products

The Danger of Nicotine Analogs

Some tobacco companies have replaced the nicotine in their e-cigarette products with nicotine analogs. Nicotine analogs are chemical compounds that are similar to nicotine in structure and target the same parts of the brain. However, because nicotine analogs are technically not nicotine, the tobacco companies argue that the FDA regulations for tobacco products no longer apply to these products. Scientists warn that there is little research on the health effects of these new nicotine-like chemicals. Mice studies suggest that nicotine analogs may be more toxic and potent than nicotine. However, human studies are still essential. "Although more research is needed, some emerging data show these nicotine analogs may be more potent than nicotine—which is already highly addictive, can alter adolescent brain development, and have long-term effects on youth's attention, learning, and memory," cautions Jim McKinney, an FDA public affairs specialist.

Pandora Dewan, "Vaping: Unregulated Chemical in New E-Cigs May Alter Brain Development," *Newsweek*, August 12, 2024. www.newsweek.com.

to teens, the federal government and some states have attempted to limit the sale of flavored vaping products by insisting that companies prove that their flavored products do not overly entice young people or nonsmokers. However, in many places across the country and especially from overseas retailers selling online, flavored vaping products are still widely available and easy for teens to get.

Regardless of why they start, nicotine dependence keeps many teens vaping. "Advertising brings the horse to water, [flavor] is what gets them to drink, and nicotine is what keeps them coming back,"[48] says King. Fourteen-year-old Jaylon Robinson from DeLand, Florida, first vaped when a friend at school suggested that he give vaping a try. Robinson says that he was hooked from the start and found it difficult to stop. "When I did not do it, I felt like I needed it, and I would get short of breath if I did not have it for a certain amount of time, and I would start to not be able to breathe," says Robinson. He adds, "Probably after the first year, I knew I was addicted."[49]

Brain Changes

More research is emerging that e-cigarettes are unsafe. For teens, the danger may be even greater. The human brain develops through a person's mid-twenties. In particular, the prefrontal cortex, the brain area responsible for decision-making, impulse control, and executive functions, continues to mature beyond the teen years. When teens vape, nicotine quickly reaches the brain. Nicotine can disrupt their brain development, especially in the synaptic connections brain cells make. "As you grow older, you do not grow more brain cells, but you grow more connections between the brain cells. Synaptic formation is hindered with nicotine use. This is where you acquire knowledge and social skill sets,"[50] explains pulmonary oncologist Pushan Jani.

Nicotine often affects brain areas that control attention, memory, and learning. It disrupts the development of attention pathways

Most teens who vape start with a flavored product, like the donut-infused e-liquids seen here.

in the brain, which can make it more difficult for teens to focus. Nicotine also affects the hippocampus, an area of the brain responsible for memory. When exposed to nicotine, the hippocampus's ability to form new memories and retain information can be impaired. Problems with attention and memory can lead to trouble in school performance and learning.

Nicotine also impacts the brain's prefrontal cortex. This area of the brain regulates impulses and is responsible for decision-making. The prefrontal cortex is still developing in teens, so some teens have less impulse control than adults with fully developed brains. However, when the brain is exposed to nicotine during this critical period, normal development can be disrupted. This disruption can lead to poor impulse control and decision-making. A person struggling with impulse control may become more likely to engage in risky and dangerous behaviors.

Mental Health

Many teens try vaping to relieve feelings of stress, anxiety, and depression. Although it might make users feel good in the short

Efforts to Reduce Youth Vaping

Mass media campaigns can be an effective way to reduce youth vaping. A 2023 study from the Truth Initiative, a nonprofit tobacco control organization, found that exposure to a weekly antivaping campaign significantly lowered youth participants' intention to vape and current use of e-cigarettes. The Truth Initiative adapted its highly successful smoking prevention programs to address youth vaping. In various videos it disseminates online, the organization pointed out that one e-cigarette juice pod contains as much nicotine as twenty tobacco cigarettes and that vaping makes it four times more likely that a young person will move on to traditional cigarette smoking. It also found that its messages that connected vaping and mental health were powerful tools to reduce e-cigarette use. The vaping prevention campaign was also successful at increasing the knowledge young people had about e-cigarettes. Young people who had seen the vaping campaign were more likely to believe that e-cigarettes were more harmful than those who had not seen the campaign.

term, vaping may worsen mental health symptoms over time. Recent research suggests that teens who vape have a higher risk of developing mental health disorders such as depression and anxiety. A 2023 survey of more than twenty-five hundred teens and young adults led by scientists at the American Heart Association found that young people who vaped were more likely to report symptoms of depression and anxiety and have suicidal thoughts as compared to nonvaping participants.

> **"Teenagers and young adults may use vaping as a coping mechanism, but doing so can deteriorate mental health and lead to addiction."[51]**
>
> —Marta De la Cruz, clinical psychologist

The study also found that many teens participated in dual vaping, a practice of using e-cigarettes with both nicotine and tetrahydrocannabinol (THC). THC is the psychoactive ingredient in marijuana. Dual vaping may be even more harmful to mental health. In studies, both nicotine and THC have been associated with anxiety and depression. Marta De la Cruz, a clinical psychologist, explains:

> Nicotine is a stimulant that may heighten alertness and arousal but also cause agitation, impatience, and anxiety. THC, on the other hand, is a cannabinoid that can trigger anxiety, paranoia, and panic attacks, in addition to relaxation and bliss. Teenagers and young adults may use vaping as a coping mechanism, but doing so can deteriorate mental health and lead to addiction.[51]

Although more research is needed, scientists suspect that nicotine and THC disrupt the developing teen brain by altering the development of areas that control motivational systems and executive functions.

A Gateway to Tobacco, Drugs, and Alcohol

There are also concerns that teen vaping is a gateway into the use of other substances, including tobacco, drugs, and alcohol. Blaha shares these concerns, saying, "I think perhaps *the* #1 concern

Studies show that young people who vape are more likely to report symptoms of depression and anxiety compared to their nonvaping counterparts.

about vaping right now is the so-called gateway effect. Our own literature suggests that 2 million young adults use electronic cigarettes as their first nicotine-based product. They're not trying to quit smoking—they've never smoked before."[52]

A 2023 study by researchers at Columbia University suggests that vaping does have a gateway effect. In the study, researchers reviewed surveys of more than fifty thousand US adolescents and analyzed responses about nicotine, cannabis, and alcohol use. They found that adolescents who vaped were more than twenty times more likely to use cannabis as compared to those who did not vape. Teens who smoked and vaped were more than forty times more likely to use cannabis compared to nonusers. Researchers also found a strong link between vaping and binge drinking. Noah Kreski, the study's lead author, explains the findings:

> Our results indicate that vaping is not an isolated behavior but rather strongly tied to other substance use that can harm adolescents and make quitting nicotine more difficult. Recognizing the strong overlap between various forms of substance use, effective intervention efforts should work to simultaneously address vaping, drinking, and cannabis use to encourage the health and well-being of young people.[53]

E-cigarettes may be a potential alternative for adult smokers who are looking to stop smoking. Most teens, however, are not long-term smokers. Many health professionals are concerned that teens will become addicted to e-cigarettes before they understand the long-term effects. "A high number of teenagers in the current generation could grow up addicted to this. It is the norm, so [teens think] surely it's appropriate or acceptable since it's trendy—only to possibly find out years later that it isn't safe and increases their risk for cancer. History has shown that—when people smoked cigarettes and thought it was perfectly safe,"[54] says Jani.

CHAPTER FIVE

Regulatory Challenges

When e-cigarettes first arrived in the United States in 2007, these products had little regulation or oversight. Manufacturers could design and market e-cigarettes as they wanted, often adding flavorings and ad campaigns that made e-cigarettes attractive to young people. As concerns grew over the potential health effects of e-cigarettes, calls for regulation grew louder.

Federal Regulation

At the time, the FDA already had regulations in place for traditional cigarettes. The Tobacco Control Act was enacted in 2009 and gave the FDA the power to regulate the manufacture, distribution, and marketing of tobacco products. Under the Tobacco Control Act, the FDA took several actions. It banned the sale and distribution of cigarettes with flavorings other than tobacco. The FDA also restricted the sale and marketing of cigarettes and smokeless tobacco to young people. Under the act, tobacco products were initially defined as cigarettes, smokeless tobacco, and roll-your-own tobacco. E-cigarettes were not included.

In 2016, the FDA extended its oversight under the Tobacco Control Act to include all tobacco products, including e-cigarettes. This gave the FDA the authority to regulate the manufacture, packaging, labeling, marketing, distribution, and sale of e-cigarettes and their components. Components included vials or pods of e-liquid, cartridges, flavorings, and batteries. The FDA initially made it illegal to sell e-cigarettes to anyone under eighteen, but in 2019 it raised the minimum age to twenty-one. It also banned sales in vending machines and the distribution of free samples. The FDA required all tobacco products, including e-cigarettes, to be labeled with warnings that they contain nicotine.

When e-cigarettes became subject to FDA tobacco regulation in 2016, these products also fell under the FDA's premarket authorization requirements. All e-cigarette products on the market must be authorized by the FDA to be legally marketed. To get this authorization, e-cigarette manufacturers were now required to submit product applications to the FDA to keep selling existing or new products. Companies were given until September 2020 to submit their applications to the FDA.

"Ultimately, the legal burden is on the [e-cigarette] companies to demonstrate that the benefit to adults is going to outweigh the harm to kids."[55]

—Mitch Zeller, director of the FDA's Center for Tobacco Products

The FDA received applications from over five hundred companies, covering millions of e-cigarette products. The FDA's review process began in 2020. The agency reviewed each e-cigarette product sold in the United States to determine if it should stay on the market or be banned. To make this decision, the agency evaluated information about the product and weighed its potential benefits as a smoking cessation aid against the public health harms it could cause, especially for young users. Mitch Zeller, director of the FDA's Center for Tobacco Products, asserts,

> It's a very fair question to ask: What is the potential benefit for adults of switching from conventional cigarettes to e-cigarettes? Especially if there's complete switching to an e-cigarette, where they can still inhale nicotine, but they're inhaling a fraction of the 7,000 chemicals that are in every puff of conventional cigarette smoke that goes into the lungs. But when it comes to kids, the harm reduction

question doesn't apply because kids should not be inhaling any of these products into their lungs. Ultimately, the legal burden is on the companies to demonstrate that the benefit to adults is going to outweigh the harm to kids.[55]

By September 2021, the agency had reviewed 93 percent of products.

As of July 2024, the FDA had approved thirty-four e-cigarette products and devices. Only products that were tobacco or menthol flavored were approved. However, critics complain that some e-cigarette products have been allowed to stay on the market for years as they wait for the FDA to complete a full review of their product applications.

Flavor Bans

E-cigarettes entice many young people with appealing mint, fruit, and dessert flavors. The federal government banned most e-cigarette flavorings in 2020 to reduce the appeal. All flavors

In the US, twenty-one is the minimum legal age to purchase vaping products. This smoke shop in Eastport, New York, clearly displays the minimum age requirement on its front door.

except menthol and tobacco were prohibited. The ban only applied to e-cigarette cartridges, which teens typically favored because they were small and easy to conceal. Flavored liquid nicotine sold at vape shops for use in open tank systems was still permitted. "By prioritizing enforcement against the products that are most widely used by children, our action today seeks to strike the right public health balance by maintaining e-cigarettes as a potential off-ramp for adults using combustible tobacco while ensuring these products don't provide an on-ramp to nicotine addiction for our youth,"[56] said Alex Azar, secretary of the US Department of Health and Human Services in 2020.

Several medical and public health organizations, including the American Medical Association (AMA), felt the ban did not go far enough to reduce youth e-cigarette use. The AMA declared, "If we are serious about tackling this epidemic and keeping these harmful products out of the hands of young people, a total ban on all flavored e-cigarettes—in all forms and at all locations—is prudent and urgently needed." It went on to add that it was "disappointed that menthol flavors—one of the most popular—will still be allowed."[57]

The Ban on Juul

Juul Labs began selling e-cigarettes in the United States in 2016. Juul products appealed to young people with an easy-to-conceal design, flashy advertising, and flavors teens liked. Within two years,

Drug Delivery Versus Tobacco Products

In 2009, the FDA attempted to halt imports of e-cigarettes. The agency argued that e-cigarettes were unapproved drug delivery devices. All drug delivery devices had to follow strict FDA guidelines. Before being sold, they had to be preapproved, registered, and listed with the FDA. However, an e-cigarette manufacturer sued the FDA, claiming that e-cigarettes should be classified as tobacco products instead of drug delivery devices because they contained nicotine. A US federal judge agreed with the manufacturer and ruled that the FDA could not halt the import of e-cigarettes and could only regulate them as tobacco products.

Juul products made up 75 percent of e-cigarette sales. Health officials raised the alarm about Juul's popularity with teens and the high nicotine content in its products.

In June 2022, the FDA banned the sale and distribution of all Juul e-cigarette products in the United States. According to Michele Mital, the acting director of the FDA's Center for Tobacco Products, the agency based its decision on Juul's lack of evidence and data to assess the health risks of its products:

> The FDA is tasked with ensuring that tobacco products sold in this country meet the standard set by the law, but the responsibility to demonstrate that a product meets those standards ultimately falls on the shoulders of the company. As with all manufacturers, Juul had the opportunity to provide evidence demonstrating that the marketing of their products meets these standards. However, the company did not provide that evidence and instead left us with significant questions.[58]

Many people concerned about the prevalence of youth vaping applauded the decision.

Juul appealed the FDA's decision, which allowed its products to remain on the market while the appeal was being reviewed. Then, in 2024, the FDA announced that it was rescinding its initial marketing ban until it reached a final decision on Juul's product marketing applications. The reversal "does not indicate whether the applications are likely to be authorized or denied," the FDA said in a statement. "The agency's continued review does not alter the fact that all e-cigarette products, including those made by JUUL, are required by law to have FDA authorization to be legally marketed."[59]

Several antivaping groups spoke out against the FDA's decision to remove its ban on Juul products pending the company's marketing applications review. "The FDA's continuing delays in

The FDA banned Juul products in 2022, but the product remains on the market pending legal appeals and review.

reviewing Juul's marketing applications are unacceptable and harmful to America's kids," asserted Yolonda C. Richardson of the Campaign for Tobacco-Free Kids. She added,

> The FDA should swiftly finish its review and again deny marketing applications for all Juul products given Juul's primary role in causing the youth e-cigarette epidemic and the continuing popularity of Juul's products among youth. There is no question that Juul fueled this epidemic by introducing a sleek, easy-to-hide product that was sold in appealing flavors, including menthol, marketed in ways that appeal to kids and delivered massive doses of nicotine that can quickly addict kids. Juul's history shows that its products are highly appealing to kids, and it cannot be trusted to act responsibly.[60]

Loopholes Lead to Mixed Results

Efforts to regulate and restrict e-cigarettes have had mixed results because of loopholes in federal regulations. For example, the FDA's 2020 ban on flavored vape pods attempted to reduce youth vaping. However, teens quickly found a loophole. The ban only covered pods designed for refillable cartridge-based vaping devices. It did not apply to disposable e-cigarettes, which are used once and thrown away. Rather than quitting, teen users turned to disposable e-cigarette brands such as Vuse and Puff Bar that could still sell candy- and dessert-flavored products. By 2021, more than 50 percent of youth reported using disposable e-cigarette products, compared to 29 percent who used refillable devices.

Daniella Roth of Newport Beach, California, is one teen who switched from refillable pods to disposable e-cigarettes. "Puff came out as the new popular thing that every single kid was doing, and I hopped on that fad," she says. "They have flavors like the Juul flavors. It's basically like smoking a Juul."[61]

E-cigarette companies also used a loophole to avoid the FDA's flavor ban. They replaced nicotine with synthetic nicotine in some

The FDA Decision Is Challenged

Two e-cigarette manufacturers, Triton Distribution and Vapetasia, challenged the FDA's denial of their e-cigarette products. Triton and Vapetasia had submitted market applications to the FDA for products with flavors, including sour grape, milk and cookies, and pink lemonade. When the FDA denied their applications, the companies sued in court. In January 2024, a federal appeals court sided with the two companies and ordered the FDA to reconsider its decision. In the court's majority opinion, Judge Andrew Oldham explained that the FDA had required the e-cigarette companies to provide detailed plans about how they would market products to prevent youth abuse and had emphasized the importance of these plans. However, the court found that the FDA denied Triton's and Vapetasia's product applications without looking at their submitted marketing plans. The court determined that the FDA had been arbitrary and capricious in its denial. The FDA appealed the decision to the US Supreme Court, which agreed in July 2024 to hear the case during its next term.

products. The FDA's authority to regulate e-cigarettes falls under its oversight of tobacco products. However, when e-cigarette companies replaced tobacco plant–based nicotine with synthetic nicotine, the product was no longer considered a tobacco product, placing it out of the FDA's reach. To close this loophole, Congress passed a law in 2022 that granted the FDA the authority to regulate tobacco products containing nicotine from any source, including synthetic nicotine.

Enforcement Efforts

To date, enforcement of federal e-cigarette regulations has been uneven. Some e-cigarette companies have continued selling products even after being rejected by the FDA. Others never applied for FDA authorization and continue to sell products.

In recent years, the FDA has increased its enforcement efforts for e-cigarette manufacturers and retailers that sell unauthorized vaping products. The agency has sent hundreds of warning letters to vape retailers and e-cigarette manufacturers, telling them to remove or discontinue the unapproved vaping products. The companies that receive a warning letter have fifteen business days to respond with how they will correct the violations. However, the warning letters are sometimes ignored. In 2023, the FDA announced the first fines against some e-cigarette manufacturers for producing and selling products without authorization. The agency has also partnered with other federal agencies to seize imports of illegal e-cigarette products.

Despite enforcement efforts, many unapproved e-cigarette products, including flavored vapes, are still widely available online and in stores. The rapidly increasing e-cigarette market is partly to blame for enforcement problems, says Kristy Marynak, a CDC senior scientist. As of 2023, there were about 260 e-cigarette brands, each of which might have thousands of different products. Technically, each product should be approved by the FDA before being sold. But in the real world, it has been too complex to enforce and easy for brands to dodge regulation. "This is an industry that is very motivated to stay in business and continue marketing products that are highly addictive and heavily flavored,"[62] says Marynak.

> **"This is an industry that is very motivated to stay in business and continue marketing products that are highly addictive and heavily flavored."[62]**
>
> **—Kristy Marynak, a CDC senior scientist**

Additionally, local police might not consider enforcement of FDA regulations to be a top priority. Nancy Heredia-Villanueva discovered that to be the case in her New Jersey community after she discovered her fourteen-year-old daughter was able to buy illegal vapes at a local gas station. Heredia-Villanueva reported the store to the local police and mayor but got little response. "I had to actually email ordinances to the detective. And even then, he was like: 'Well, what am I supposed to do about it?'"[63] she says.

Officers remove bags of cigarette cartons and vape products that they found at an unlicensed store in Brooklyn, New York, on August 1, 2024.

State and Local Regulations

Several states and local communities have passed laws and ordinances that regulate e-cigarettes. Some have restricted the sale of flavored tobacco products, including e-cigarettes. Many have imposed taxes on the sale of e-cigarette products.

Seventeen states—as well as Washington, DC, and Puerto Rico—have banned e-cigarettes indoors under smoke-free indoor air laws. These laws ban smoking any type of cigarette, including using e-cigarettes in indoor spaces such as restaurants, bars, and private workplaces.

E-cigarettes have been promoted as a healthier alternative to smoking. However, e-cigarettes are not risk-free. As experts learn more about e-cigarettes, concerns about health and addiction risks, especially for teens and young adults, have grown. As a result, calls for regulation of e-cigarettes have grown louder. About 60 percent of Americans want stricter vaping regulations, according to a 2022 Gallup poll. However, any regulation must balance the potential benefit of e-cigarettes as smoking cessation tools against the potential harm, especially for the youngest users.

SOURCE NOTES

Introduction: A Vaping Habit

1. Quoted in John Daley, "Young Adults Who Started Vaping as Teens Still Can't Shake the Habit," *Morning Edition*, National Public Radio, April 9, 2024. www.npr.org.
2. Quoted in Daley, "Young Adults Who Started Vaping as Teens Still Can't Shake the Habit."
3. Quoted in Daley, "Young Adults Who Started Vaping as Teens Still Can't Shake the Habit."
4. Quoted in Rob Stein, "Surgeon General Warns Youth Vaping Is Now An 'Epidemic,'" *Shots* (blog), National Public Radio, December 18, 2018. www.npr.org.

Chapter One: An Alternative to Cigarettes

5. Quoted in Stop Smoking London, "Success Stories: I Swapped Cigarettes for Vaping After My Wife Died." https://stopsmokinglondon.com.
6. Quoted in Stop Smoking London, "Success Stories."
7. Quoted in Stop Smoking London, "Success Stories."
8. Quoted in Stop Smoking London, "Success Stories."
9. Allison Boughner, "From Despair to Hope: How Vaping Saved My Life and Gave Me a Second Chance," World Vapers' Alliance, October 10, 2024. https://worldvapersalliance.com.
10. Clive D. Bates, "Point: E-Cigarette Use for Harm Reduction in Tobacco Use Disorder? Yes," *Chest*, vol. 160, no. 3, September 2021, pp. 807–9. https://doi.org/10.1016/j.chest.2021.04.046.
11. Quoted in Leslie Cantu, "Largest US Study of E-Cigarettes Shows Their Value as Smoking Cessation Aid," Hollings Cancer Center, Medical University of South Carolina, August 18, 2023. https://hollingscancercenter.musc.edu.
12. Quoted in Kenneth E. Warner et al., "Nicotine E-Cigarettes as a Tool for Smoking Cessation," *Nature Medicine*, February 2023. https://doi.org/10.1038/s41591-022-02201-7.
13. Quoted in Yadira Galindo, "Studies: E-Cigarettes Don't Help Smokers Quit and They May Become Addicted to Vaping," UC San Diego Health, September 2, 2020. https://health.ucsd.edu.
14. Quoted in Galindo, "Studies."
15. Quoted in Kelsey Hudnall, "Most US Adults Who Vape Want to Quit, Study Finds," Hollings Cancer Center, Medical University of South Carolina, April 2, 2021. https://hollingscancercenter.musc.edu.

16. Quoted in Hudnall, "Most US Adults Who Vape Want to Quit, Study Finds."

Chapter Two: Nicotine Addiction

17. Quoted in Abbie Jones, "Vaping: E-Cigarettes Have Ruined My Life, Woman Says," BBC News, June 24, 2023. www.bbc.com.
18. Quoted in Jones, "Vaping."
19. Quoted in Liz Szabo, "Sales of E-Cigs Packed with Nicotine Soar as Regulators Try to Crack Down," NBC News, June 21, 2023. www.nbcnews.com.
20. Quoted in Susanne Pallo, "New Studies Suggest Vaping Could Cloud Your Thoughts," University of Rochester Medical Center, December 28, 2020. www.urmc.rochester.edu.
21. Francesco Versace, "Vaping and Your Brain: What to Know," University of Texas MD Anderson Cancer Center, April 19, 2024. www.mdanderson.org.
22. Versace, "Vaping and Your Brain."
23. Quoted in University of Surrey, "Vaping Worsens Sleep Quality and the Mental Health of Young People," press release, March 5, 2024. www.surrey.ac.uk.
24. Quoted in University of Surrey, "Vaping Worsens Sleep Quality and the Mental Health of Young People."
25. Quoted in Szabo, "Sales of E-Cigs Packed with Nicotine Soar as Regulators Try to Crack Down."
26. Quoted in Szabo, "Sales of E-Cigs Packed with Nicotine Soar as Regulators Try to Crack Down."
27. Quoted in Clea Skopeliti, "'Beside Himself with Craving': The Teenagers Hooked on Vaping," *The Guardian*, March 18, 2023. www.theguardian.com.

Chapter Three: The Impact on Health

28. Quoted in Editorial Staff, "'I Almost Died': A Vaping Horror Story," *Each Breath* (blog), American Lung Association, May 8, 2024. www.lung.org.
29. Quoted in Editorial Staff, "'I Almost Died.'"
30. Quoted in Editorial Staff, "'I Almost Died.'"
31. Quoted in Regan Olsson, "Vaping vs. Smoking: Why One Isn't Better than the Other," *Teach Me* (blog), Banner Health, January 31, 2022. www.bannerhealth.com.
32. Quoted in Olsson, "Vaping vs. Smoking."
33. Quoted in National Heart, Lung, and Blood Institute, "NIH-Funded Studies Show Damaging Effects of Vaping, Smoking on Blood Vessels," National Institutes of Health, October 26, 2022. www.nih.gov.

34. Quoted in National Heart, Lung, and Blood Institute, "NIH-Funded Studies Show Damaging Effects of Vaping, Smoking on Blood Vessels."
35. Quoted in National Heart, Lung, and Blood Institute, "NIH-Funded Studies Show Damaging Effects of Vaping, Smoking on Blood Vessels."
36. Quoted in Corrie Pelc, "Vaping, Even Once, May Raise the Risk of Heart Failure, Study Finds," MedicalNewsToday, April 27, 2024. www.medicalnewstoday.com.
37. Quoted in Olsson, "Vaping vs. Smoking."
38. Quoted in Stephen R. Broderick, "What Does Vaping Do to Your Lungs?," Johns Hopkins Medicine. www.hopkinsmedicine.org.
39. Quoted in Erika Edwards, "E-Cigarettes Linked to Lung Problems, First Long-Term Study on Vaping Finds," NBC News, December 16, 2019. www.nbcnews.com.
40. Quoted in The James, "Young Vapers at Risk for Respiratory Symptoms, Regardless of Whether or Not They Smoke Other Products," Ohio State University Comprehensive Cancer Center, August 16, 2023. https://cancer.osu.edu.
41. Quoted in University of North Carolina School of Medicine, "UNC Researchers Tackle the E-Cigarette or Vaping Product Use-Associated Lung Injury (EVALI) Epidemic," January 3, 2023. https://news.unchealthcare.org.

Chapter Four: Youth and Vaping

42. Quoted in News.com.au, "Teen Became Addicted to Vaping at Just 14 Years Old," *New York Post,* October 20, 2022. www.nypost.com.
43. Quoted in News.com.au, "Teen Became Addicted to Vaping at Just 14 Years Old."
44. Quoted in News.com.au, "Teen Became Addicted to Vaping at Just 14 Years Old."
45. Quoted in Centers for Disease Control and Prevention, "Youth E-Cigarette Use Drops to Lowest Level in a Decade," September 5, 2024. www.cdc.gov.
46. Quoted in Centers for Disease Control and Prevention, "Youth E-Cigarette Use Drops to Lowest Level in a Decade."
47. Quoted in Johns Hopkins Medicine, "5 Vaping Facts You Need to Know." www.hopkinsmedicine.org.
48. Quoted in Jennifer Thomas, "Why Do So Many Teens Vape?," Rally Health, April 24, 2020. www.rallyhealth.com.
49. Quoted in Randy Rauch, "Teen Uses Own Addiction to Warn Others About Vaping," Spectrum News 13, March 14, 2023. https://mynews13.com.

50. Quoted in Vicki Powers, "The Reality for Teens Who Vape," University of Texas Health Science Center at Houston, November 14, 2023. www.utphysicians.com.
51. Quoted in Tony Hicks, "How Vaping Nicotine and THC May Increase Depression, Anxiety in Teens," Healthline, February 28, 2023. www.healthline.com.
52. Quoted in Johns Hopkins Medicine, "Will Vaping Lead Teens to Smoking Cigarettes?" www.hopkinsmedicine.org.
53. Quoted in Katherine Keyes, "Is Vaping New Gateway into Further Substance Use?," Mailman School of Public Health, Columbia University, May 19, 2023. www.publichealth.columbia.edu.
54. Quoted in Powers, "The Reality for Teens Who Vape."

Chapter Five: Regulatory Challenges

55. Quoted in Carmen Phillips, "FDA Oversight of E-Cigarettes Gathers Speed: A Conversation with Mitch Zeller," National Cancer Institute, January 5, 2022. www.cancer.gov.
56. Quoted in Abby Goodnough, Maggie Haberman, and Sheila Kaplan, "With Partial Flavor Ban, Trump Splits the Difference on Vaping," *New York Times*, February 12, 2020. www.nytimes.com.
57. Quoted in Goodnough, Haberman, and Kaplan, "With Partial Flavor Ban, Trump Splits the Difference on Vaping."
58. Quoted in Aria Bendix and Dana Varinsky, "FDA Orders Juul to Stop Selling E-Cigarette Products," NBC News, June 23, 2022. www.nbcnews.com.
59. Quoted in Carma Hassan and Jen Christensen, "FDA Rescinds Marketing Ban on Juul Vaping Products," CNN, June 6, 2024. www.cnn.com.
60. Yolonda C. Richardson, "FDA's Continued Delays in Reviewing Juul's Marketing Applications Are Unacceptable and Harmful to Kids," Campaign for Tobacco-Free Kids, June 6, 2024. www.tobaccofreekids.org.
61. Quoted in Sheila Kaplan, "Teens Find a Big Loophole in the New Flavored Vaping Ban," *New York Times*, January 31, 2020. www.nytimes.com.
62. Quoted in Yuki Noguchi, "They're Illegal. So Why Is It So Easy to Buy the Disposable Vapes Favored by Teens?," *Shots* (blog), National Public Radio, July 14, 2023. www.npr.org.
63. Quoted in Noguchi, "They're Illegal."

FOR FURTHER RESEARCH

Books

John Allen, *Thinking Critically: E-Cigarettes and Vaping*. San Diego, CA: ReferencePoint, 2023.

Eric Benac, *Deadly Vaping Additives: CBD, THC, and Contaminants*. Philadelphia, PA: Mason Crest, 2022.

Eric Benac, *Vaping: The New Cool Way to a Shorter Life*. Philadelphia, PA: Mason Crest, 2022.

Terri Dougherty, *Vaping: Considering the Risks*. San Diego, CA: ReferencePoint, 2022.

Hilary W. Poole, *Smoking and Vaping*. Hollywood, FL: Mason Crest, 2023.

Internet Sources

Stephen R. Broderick, "What Does Vaping Do to Your Lungs?," Johns Hopkins Medicine. www.hopkinsmedicine.org.

Campaign for Tobacco-Free Kids, "Electronic Cigarettes: An Overview of Key Issues." https://assets.tobaccofreekids.org/factsheets/0379.pdf.

Callie Holtermann, "Vapes Get a Gen Z Makeover," *New York Times*, November 6, 2023. www.nytimes.com.

Christina Jewett, "Teenage E-Cigarette Use Drops to a 10-Year Low," *New York Times*, September 5, 2024. www.nytimes.com.

Christina Jewett, "Teenagers Keep Vaping Despite Crackdowns on E-Cigarettes," *New York Times*, October 6, 2022. www.nytimes.com.

Puja Khaitan, "Vaping to Quit Smoking? Here's the Truth about E-Cigarettes," MedStar Health, September 9, 2022. www.medstarhealth.org.

Sarah Moore, "Vaping vs. Smoking: Is One Really Safer than the Other?," News Medical, October 17, 2023. www.news-medical.net.

Organizations and Websites

American Lung Association

www.lung.org

The American Lung Association strives to improve lung health and prevent lung disease through education, advocacy, and research. Its website has information about vaping and lung health.

Campaign for Tobacco-Free Kids
www.tobaccofreekids.org
The Campaign for Tobacco-Free Kids is a leading advocacy organization working to reduce tobacco use, including e-cigarettes, in the United States and worldwide. Its website has the latest news, information, and research about e-cigarettes.

Centers for Disease Control and Prevention (CDC)
www.cdc.gov
The CDC is the premier public health agency in the United States. Its website includes government-vetted information about nicotine, e-cigarettes, and smoking.

Truth Initiative
https://truthinitiative.org
The Truth Initiative is a nonprofit public health organization. It works to prevent nicotine addiction among young people and to help current users quit. Its website has information and research related to vaping.

US Food and Drug Administration (FDA)
www.fda.gov
The FDA is a federal agency in the US Department of Health and Human Services. It is responsible for protecting public health by ensuring the safety of the US food supply, drugs, and other products. It has information about tobacco products on its website, including public education materials, science and research, and the latest regulations.

World Health Organization (WHO)
www.who.int
The WHO is an agency of the United Nations responsible for international public health. The WHO works to promote health for people by conducting research, providing support to local health agencies, and monitoring worldwide health trends. It has information and fact sheets about several health topics, including tobacco, on its website.

INDEX

Note: Boldface page numbers indicate illustrations.